CARRIE HEPPLE'S GARDEN

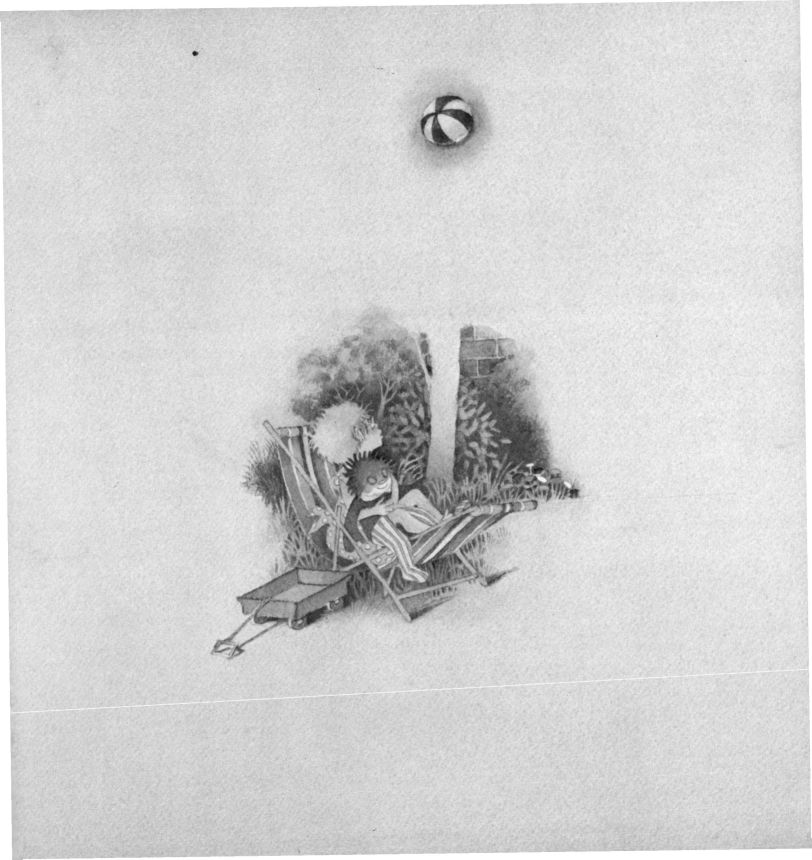

CARRIE HEPPLE'S GARDEN

GARDEN

RUTH CRAFT
Illustrated by IRENE HAAS

A MARGARET K. MC ELDERRY BOOK

Atheneum   1979   New York

Library of Congress Cataloging in Publication Data
Craft, Ruth.
Carrie Hepple's garden.
"A Margaret K. McElderry book."
SUMMARY: Three children venture into eccentric
Carrie Hepple's garden in search of their ball
and learn some strange and unexpected things.
[1. Stories in rhyme] I. Haas, Irene.
II. Title.
PZ8.3.C842Car   [E]   78-397
ISBN 0-689-50099-8

Text copyright © 1979 by Ruth Craft
Illustrations copyright © 1979 by Irene Haas
All rights reserved
Library of Congress catalog card number 78-397
ISBN 0-068-50099-8
Published simultaneously in Canada by
McClelland & Stewart, Ltd.
Manufactured in the United States of America by
Eastern Press, Inc., New Haven Connecticut
Bound by The Book Press, Brattleboro, Vermont
First American Edition

For my Father, Geoffrey T. Alley

Midsummer evening.
The light is soft
and the air is warm.
They're playing ball on the tidy lawn,
throwing it over, under and back,
when suddenly
smack!
The ball sails over the wall
into *Carrie Hepple's garden!*

Carrie Hepple's garden!

"We can't go in there!"

Carrie Hepple has a glittering glare

and whiskery hair.

She's been seen in her garden

late at night

with a cake tin and milk

and a shadowy light.

Someone heard her saying,

"Come on, *Old Sausage!* It's all right!"

Carrie Hepple's garden!
A muddle of jungle and tangle.
And lost toys galore
must lie unlooked for there.
For who'd dare face Carrie Hepple's stare?
Who'd knock at her door?

She'd *roar!*
One is brave in the shadows,
the smallest, come to that.
She finds a broken slat
and squeezes through.
Then the others come, too.

"Ouch!"
"Ssssh!"
"There's a piece of long grass down my back!"
"Oh crikey! What's that?"
"Carrie Hepple's cat!"

Still, sleek and lounging.
(They say he's always scrounging.)
Not a strokable cat —
too old, too growly and spitty
for nonsense like that.
His eyes, green and golden,
watch them pass,
as they wriggle and rustle
through the long dusty grass.

"There's the ball!"
"Where?"
"Over there by the rose."
Quickly, softly, on tippy-toes,
they reach forward to fetch it.
"Bend down! Keep low, do!"
"Oh! somebody's shoe!"

Carrie Hepple's shoe!
And her other shoe,
her legs and her dress
and her whiskery hair.
"And what, may I ask,"
says Carrie Hepple,
"are *you* doing here?"

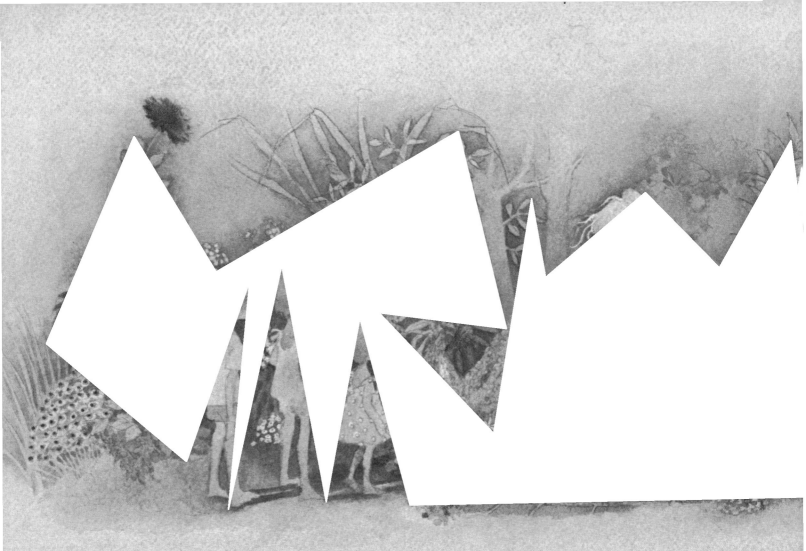

"We've come for our ball. That's all."
"Ah!" says Carrie Hepple.
"Well, since you're passing through,
allow me to show you
a curiosity or two."

("A curiosity? What's that?"

"I'll bet it's just that spitty old cat.")

"Oh no, let's go!"

"Better not, she said stay.

She might magic us back if we all run away."

"Follow me," calls Carrie Hepple.
They follow and stop,
but what's there to see?
Not a lot.
Just a pot of tumbling, trumpet nasturtium flowers.
Carrie Hepple says nothing for what seems like hours,
so they look at her feet.
Then she speaks.
"It's a curiosity to me,
and it may be to you,
that the seeds of nasturtiums came to the
gardens of England
in 1582. From Peru."

(One whispered,
"I'd rather be in Peru
than in this garden,
wouldn't you?")

"Now look sharp right!" calls Carrie Hepple.
They spin round smartly and see a sight
that must be magical, for it can't be true
that green mist is rising round stars of blue.
But Carrie Hepple says they're flowers.
"*Nigella damascena,*
but the old name will do —
'Love-in-a-mist.'
The green is the mist,
and the love is the blue."
They notice how carefully
the green holds the blue.

There's a trip and a crash,
the din of a tin
and a milky splash.
"Oh drat!" says Carrie Hepple.
"Look at that.
Old Sausage's milk has gone west.
Phew! Probably for the best.
It's gone sour in the heat,
and sour milk is no treat.
Who is Old Sausage?
Well, come along now, *think!*
What's a shy and prickly beast
that likes a milky midnight drink?"

(Oh, of course, they think.
That's right. Hedgehogs come out in the dark of night.
And they'd like a drink, and you'd need a light.)

The sun has gone.
A little wind begins to blow.
"And now," says Carrie Hepple,
"you must go. But before you do,
have something to chew.
A hermit.
They're kept
in the crock by the door.
You may have four."

(A *hermit!*
A hermit's an old man
who lives all alone!
Does Carrie Hepple keep them
locked in a crock of stone?)

Carrie Hepple takes off the top
of the crock.
They can't bear to look,
but an orangey smell of spices rare
whiffs and wafts
through the summer air.

"A hermit's the name of a special bun,"
says Carrie Hepple.
"I make them occasionally, for fun.
Off you go now, there's good people."

"Good-bye and thank you, Carrie Hepple."

Back on the tidy lawn.

"It wasn't so bad after all,

but after all that
we forgot the ball!"

"Mind your eyeglass!"
A voice calls from over the wall,

and the ball comes back, flying as high as a steeple.
"Oh thank you, thank you, Carrie Hepple."